Sea O

Series "Fun Facts on Water Animals for Kids"

Written by Michelle Hawkins

Sea Otter

Series "Fun Facts on Ocean Animals for Kids"
By: Michelle Hawkins
Version 1.1 ~August 2021
Published by Michelle Hawkins at KDP
Copyright ©2021 by Michelle Hawkins. All rights reserved.

No part of this publication may be reproduced, distributed or transmitted in any form or by any means including photocopying, recording or other electronic or mechanical methods or by any information storage or retrieval system without the prior written permission of the publishers, except in the case of very brief quotations embodied in critical reviews and certain other noncommercial uses permitted by copyright law.

All rights reserved, including the right of reproduction in whole or in part in any form.

All information in this book has been carefully researched and checked for factual accuracy. However, the author and publisher make no warranty, express or implied, that the information contained herein is appropriate for every individual, situation, or purpose and assume no responsibility for errors or omissions.

The reader assumes the risk and full responsibility for all actions. The author will not be held responsible for any loss or damage, whether consequential, incidental, special or otherwise, that may result from the information presented in this book.

All images are free for use or purchased from stock photo sites or royalty-free for commercial use. I have relied on my own observations as well as many different sources for this book, and I have done my best to check facts and give credit where it is due. In the event that any material is used without proper permission, please contact me so that the oversight can be corrected.

There are one million hairs of fur on each square inch of a Sea Otter's body.

Sea Otters are considered threatened.

Sea Otters help to control the Sea Urchin population.

The head and chest on a Sea Otter are lighter in color than the rest of the body.

Mom will lick the baby Sea Otter so much that their fur will float due to air bubbles.

Sea Otters are known as the Old Man of the Sea.

Sea Otters use their fur to keep them warm because they have no blubber as other sea animals do.

Sea Otters will clap to help their hands and feet stay out of the water.

Sea Otters are primarily found in Canada, Russia, and the United States.

The back feet of Sea Otters are shaped like flippers.

Male Sea Otters stay with other males, and females remain with other female Sea Otters.

Sea Otters use seaweed as a raft to avoid floating away.

Sea Otters use rocks to help them when hunting for food to eat.

Sea Otters are part of the Mustelidae family.

The fur on a Sea Otter helps to repel water.

Sea Otters will use rocks to help them open the shell on food.

Sea Otter's favorite thing to eat is Sea Urchins.

The fur on a Sea Otter is known as Lanugo.

The average life span of a Sea Otter is between ten to twenty years.

Mom will carry the baby Sea Otter on her chest when floating or sleeping.

Sea Otters are considered very playful among themselves.

Sea Otters sleep on their backs in the water.

When diving, Sea Otters will use their whiskers and paws to help find food.

Baby Sea Otters get their adult fur at 13 weeks of age.

Sea Otters weigh between 30 to 100 pounds.

Each day a Sea Otter will eat 25% of its weight in food.

Sea Otters are related to the weasels.

Sea Otters have two pairs of lower incisor teeth.

Sea Otters will hold hands with each other to avoid drifting while sleeping.

A group of Sea Otters on land is called a romp.

Sea Otters can dive up to 300 feet.

The teeth on a Sea Otter can open up a clam.

Sea Otters are constantly eating, grooming, or sleeping.

The tail of a Sea Otter is very muscular.

Baby Sea Otters will stay with their mother for up to twelve months.

The fur on a Sea Otter is so thick so that no water will get on its skin.

Sea Otters are carnivores with their favorite foods clams, crabs, fish, sea urchins, and snails.

Sea Otters are known to have strong teeth.

The sleek body of a Sea Otter is excellent for swimming and diving.

Sea Otters enjoy floating on their back.

Sea Otters can swim up to seven miles per hour.

When born, Sea Otters have 26 teeth.

The female life span of a Sea Otter is 15 to 20 years.

Sea Otters will store food underneath their arm.

Sea Otters use their paws to help dig for clams.

Sea Otters can hold their breath for up to five minutes.

The fur on a Sea Otter is water-resistant.

Sea Otters have been known to juggle rocks.

Sea Otters have very dense fur.

Sea Otters wrap themselves in kelp to avoid floating away while sleeping.

The fingers on a Sea Otter are very flexible.

Sea Otter's colors are black, brown, gray, and silver.

90% of all Sea Otters live off the coast of Alaska.

Sea Otters are known to have a powerful bite.

Sea Otters can dive five miles per hour.

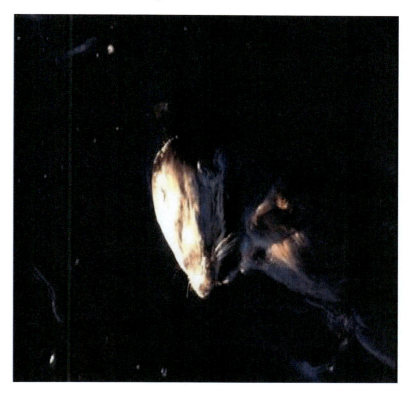

It is hard for Sea Otters to see when in deep water.

Sea Otters enjoy being in the open ocean.

Sea Otters can range in size from 39 to 63 inches long.

Sea Otters communicate with each other through contact and sounds.

When Sea Otters swim underwater, their nose is shut off, so no water goes in.

The tail of a Sea Otter makes up 30% of its body.

The predators of a Sea Otter are humans, sharks, and whales.

There are thirteen different types of Otters.

Most food for Sea Otters is found within sixty feet below the water's surface.

Sea Otters have a high metabolism.

It is rare for female Sea Otters to have twins.

Sea Otters can float easily in water.

By rubbing Sea Otter's fur, it helps them with insulation and puts air in their fur.

Half of a Sea Otter's day is spent grooming themselves.

Sea Otters walk on land awkwardly.

A group of Sea Otters is called a raft.

Sea Otter's whiskers will vibrate when they are looking for food.

Sea Otters are part of the Weasel family.

A baby Sea Otter is called a pup.

No mammal has thicker fur than a Sea Otter.

The tail of a Sea Otter is flat.

Every year on the last week of September is considered Sea Otter week.

Sea Otters never have to leave the water if they choose not to.

Sea Otters are found mainly in the Northern Pacific Ocean.

Baby Sea Otters can swim at four weeks old.

Sea Otters are great at smell and taste.

The average life span of a male Sea Otter is between ten to fifteen years old.

Sea Otters are very social creatures.

Sea Otters are very skillful with their hands.

Sea Otters will put food on their stomach to eat it.

Sea Otters are mammals.

Sea Otter is the biggest type of Otter.

Find me on Amazon at:

https://amzn.to/3oqoXoG

and on Facebook at:

https://bit.ly/3ovFJ5V

Other Books by Michelle Hawkins

Series

Fun Facts on Birds for Kids.

Fun Fact on Fruits and Vegetables

Fun Facts on Small Animals

Fun Facts on Dogs for Kids.

Fun Facts on Dates for Kids.

Fun Facts on Zoo Animals for Kids

Fun Facts on Farm Animals for Kids

Fun Facts on Ocean Animals for Kids.

10% of all profits are donated to World Vision at https://rb.gy/cahrb0

Printed in Great Britain
by Amazon

83535561R00020